Cats

Cats

Judith Steeh

Bison Books

This edition published in the USA for
K Mart Corporation
Troy, Michigan 48084

Copyright © 1983 Bison Books Corp.

Produced by Bison Books Corp.
17 Sherwood Place
Greenwich, CT 06830, USA

ISBN 0 86124 093 6

Printed in Hong Kong

PAGE 2: *The Smoke Persian, sometimes called the Smoke Long-hair. The dense, silky coat requires frequent grooming to remove loose hairs and keep it looking its best; the coat should be brushed away from the body. Smoke Persian kittens are born black.* THIS PAGE, ABOVE: *The Chocolate Point Himalayan. Himalayan cats are sometimes called Colorpoint Long-hairs. It is the fastest growing breed in the world today, combining Persian conformation and coat quality with Siamese colors and patterns.* RIGHT: *The Russian Blue. It is thought that sailors brought the breed from Archangel, Russia to England, and, in fact, it was called the Archangel Cat for many years. It is said to have also been a treasured pet of the Tsars of Russia.*

Contents

Cats in History

Origins

Cats, or *Felidae*, are found throughout the world, but all – big or small, wild or domesticated – have so much in common that scientists have not formally subdivided them. This and other evidence strongly suggests that all cats had a common ancestor.

The first cats appeared in the Oligocene era, about 20 million years ago. There were two types: one, *Holophoneus*, produced *Smilodon*, the saber-tooth tiger and the other, *Dimictis*, eventually evolved into the modern day cat.

Dimictis was smaller than *Holophoneus*, faster, more agile, and much more intelligent. This, then was the ancestor of the almost 40 different cat species recognized today.

No one knows how or when domestic cats appeared on the scene. They are almost certainly mixtures of several species of wild cat (in scientific terms they are of *polyphyletic origin*). The earliest records state that domestic cats came from Egypt and are only about 5000 years old (dogs have been domesticated for at least 20,000 years). Short-haired cats were exported from Egypt to the European continent by the Phoenicians and to the New World by European colonists.

Ancient Egypt

The heyday of the domestic cat was certainly in ancient Egypt, where the pets were not only useful members of society, but for almost 2000 years were deified as well.

The fertile Nile Valley was the granary of the ancient world, and rats and mice must have caused severe damage before the cat appeared on the scene. In addition, cats were trained to hunt snakes, birds, and other small mammals, and even to retrieve ducks for hunters.

No one knows exactly why or when the Egyptian cat came to play such an important role in religion, but probably the reason for its deification was a complex mixture of respect for its hunting abilities, love of its beauty, and awe of its mysterious 'magical' personality. Paintings, sculptures, and tomb decorations portray a short-haired elegant cat very similar in size and shape to today's Abyssinian.

The cat goddess Bastet (or Bast or Pasht) was the daughter of Isis (goddess of the sun, moon, and earth) and Ra (god of the sun and the underworld). Worship of Bastet (and her representative, the cat) reached its peak around 950 BC. Beginning as the goddess of sexuality and fertility, she became the sun, moon, motherhood, and love goddess as well, in addition to protecting the dead, decreeing the success or failure of crops, making rain, and helping heal the sick, especially children.

OPPOSITE: An ancient Egyptian Bronze cast about 600 BC.
BELOW: An Abyssinian kitten. These cats were once known as 'Bunny' or 'Rabbit' cats because of their fur.

8

More than 700,000 pilgrims traveled by boat to Bubastis each spring for her festival which was the gayest of the year. The appearance of the boats loaded with singing, dancing people was a signal to those who remained at home in cities along the way to begin their own festival.

Although there are several accurate accounts of the pilgrims' journey to Bubastis, no one seems to know exactly what went on when they got there. Some historians limit the attractions to good music, food, and wine while others describe the festival as a huge drunken sexual orgy. There were, at any rate, many parades, and the atmosphere was probably very like that at Mardi Gras or Oktoberfest.

Egyptian cats had either short ears and blunt noses or long ears and sharp noses. Most were short-haired and ginger-colored with black markings. They were spoiled and pampered by peasant and pharaoh alike; mummified cats have been found wearing necklaces, earrings, and even nose rings. When they died cats were given elaborate funerals, and the household where the death occurred was plunged into deepest mourning. Even poor families held a wake for their pet, and the bereaved owners shaved their eyebrows to demonstrate their grief.

For a long time it was illegal to harm a cat in Egypt, and the crime was punishable by death. Herodotus, who was usually quite accurate about things he saw firsthand (if a bit credulous when it came to believing other travelers' stories), gives a graphic description of an unfortunate Egyptian who happened to witness the death of a cat – trembling, bathed in tears, loudly proclaiming to all and sundry that he had had no part in the matter. Perhaps there was good reason for this extreme behavior – one Roman soldier was literally torn to pieces by an infuriated mob in Thebes after he accidentally killed a cat.

By about 100 BC cat worship was in decline and Phoenician traders, who had been trying for years to smuggle cats to a rodent-ridden world, were finally able to export them in quantity. The best days had come to an end.

LEFT: *The Egyptian Mau is the only domesticated (natural breed) spotted cat, and it was developed in the 1950s from cats imported from Cairo, Egypt. It is a modern-day counterpart of the cats that can be seen in a 3500-year-old frieze in an ancient tomb in Thebes. The frieze shows a hunting scene in which a spotted cat is stalking ducks for an Egyptian hunter.*

Europe

By the end of the fifth century AD the domestic cat was well established in the Middle East and Europe. As the barbaric invasions brought rats and plague sweeping across the continent, cats rose in value. In several countries in fact (including Wales and Switzerland), there were laws governing the sale and protection of cats.

Unfortunately, during the Dark Ages the cat became an outcast. Cats never quite lost the supernatural, pagan reputation they had acquired in Egypt, and they were soon caught up in a wave of witch-hunting and persecutions. There are horror stories by the dozen of cats – hundreds of thousands of them – being burned, flayed, crucified, and thrown from the tops of towers, usually under the auspices of the Church.

Paradoxically, the cat was saved by the Black Death. Returning Crusaders brought with them the Asiatic black rat, carrier of the bubonic plague. With so few cats left the rats bred unhindered, and in only two years in the middle of the fourteenth century three out of every four people in Europe died of the disease. Those who had sometimes literally risked their lives to keep cats now came into their own; their homes and farms were relatively free from

rats. Gradually the authorities saw the light and ended their persecution.

By the end of the Renaissance cats were again valued members of society. Cardinal Wolsey in England insisted on taking his cat with him to the cathedral and to royal conferences. In France Montaigne, Richelieu, and Mazarin all doted on their pets, and Moncrif wrote his charming *Histoire des Chats*, the first cat book as we know it.

The Victorian Age found the cat prized not only as a useful pet, but as a thing of beauty. Cats were fashionable; the first cat show was held at Crystal Palace in London in 1871. In 1895 an American version was held at Madison Square Garden, and the success of these shows began a tradition that continues to this day.

BELOW: A close-up of the Black Short-hair cat. OPPOSITE: A full portrait of the Black Short-hair. This is the cat associated with the Devil and witchcraft in more superstitious times. Today black cats are still regarded with lingering misgivings in America and Ireland, but in Britain they have come to be thought of as lucky cats. Constant grooming is necessary to avoid rusty patches in their coats.

11

The sturdy Chartreux is the extremely common Blue Short-hair of France, and it is thought to have been brought to that country from South Africa by Carthusian monks. It is a gentle, affectionate and intelligent animal, and it is also a skilled hunter of rodents. Its confirmation and coloring are essentially the same as the British Blue cat.

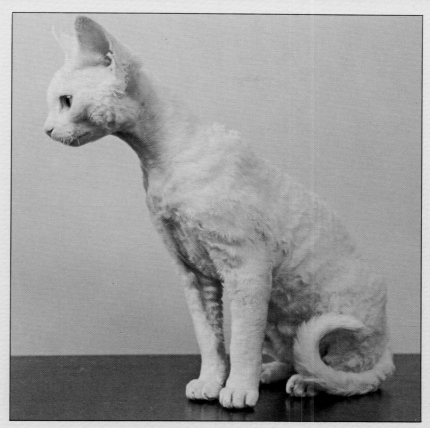

LEFT: *The Rex, a spontaneous mutation of the domestic cat. Its short, tightly curled coat gives it an exotic appearance that appeals to many. Many people who are allergic to cat hairs find the Rex, because of its special coat, the perfect pet. The first Rex was discovered in 1950 in Cornwall, England. It was bred back to its dam, resulting in several curly-coated kittens. Eventually its bloodline was established.* ABOVE: *An adult Devon Rex.*

The New World

Domestic cats probably arrived in the Americas with Columbus or shortly thereafter – there were certainly only wild cats in the New World before it was colonized by Europeans.

In the early part of the eighteenth century cats traveled with the Jesuits as they moved up the west coast of Mexico. There were cats on the *Mayflower*, and in the middle of the seventeenth century many more were imported to help defeat a horde of black rats who were battling the colonists for their grain supplies.

Cats traveled with the French voyageurs on the great Midwestern waterways, and pushed westward with the wagon trains. As the Indians discovered the cat's hunting abilities the animals became valuable trading items, and later western miners paid as much as fifty dollars for a good mouser.

The Orient

Domestic cats probably arrived in China early in the Han dynasty (206 BC–221 AD) and were soon firmly entrenched in Chinese society.

The first known litter of kittens in Japan was born on 19 September 999 in the Imperial Palace in Kyoto. It was the Emperor Ichijo's thirteenth birthday and he was so completely entranced by the small animals that he ordered the kittens to be given the same care that royal infants usually received.

For several centuries cats in Japan belonged exclusively to royalty. But around the fourteenth century the growing silk industry was threatened by mice. Cats, who were by then more numerous, became even more valuable and closely guarded. Finally the authorities were forced to decree that all cats were to be set loose, and that it was forbidden to buy or sell them.

Today cats are highly regarded in both China and Japan – in the former, more for their prowess in hunting rodents, and in the latter perhaps more for their beauty and charm.

The Abyssinian (or 'Aby') is sometimes called the Cat from the Blue Nile and has long been thought to resemble the sacred cats of ancient Egypt.

Cats in Folklore and Myth

The larger members of the cat family appear in the myths and legends of almost every country in the world, and the domestic cat too, has a place in that tradition.

There were no domestic cats in Eden – only lions, tigers, panthers, and leopards – and in fact the Bible does not mention cats at all (perhaps because they were being worshiped as pagan gods in nearby Egypt at roughly the time the Bible was being written). But legend has it that during the long weeks afloat in the Ark the rat and mouse population increased so alarmingly that the rodents soon threatened the safety of the entire ship. Noah, rising to the occasion, passed his hand three times over the head of the lioness, and she obligingly sneezed forth a cat who soon dealt with the problem.

The ancient Greeks had another story of the cat's creation – one of the few times the animals are mentioned in their literature. Apollo, it seems, created the lion and sent it to frighten his sister Diana. The Huntress was not so easily intimidated however, and promptly created the domestic cat as a parody to poke fun at her brother's monster. Diana was also goddess of the moon, an association cats had held earlier in Egypt and retained for centuries thereafter.

According to an old Norse legend, Utgard-Loki, king of the giants, had a giant cat; and of course Freyya, goddess of love and marriage, rode in a chariot pulled by two cats.

Cats hold a special place in the Arab world, as Selema held a special place in Mohammed's heart. It is written that once in Damascus the prophet cut off his sleeve rather than disturb his sleeping cat when it was time for prayers. A Sultan in Cairo was the first man known to have left a legacy for stray cats. Cats figure in several tales in the *Arabian Nights*, and Burton claims that the word 'tabby' comes from a quarter of Baghdad called Attabi that is famous for its watered or streaked silks.

LEFT: A Brown Tabby Persian (Long-hair) kitten. Note the copper eyes and classic markings. The term 'Tabby' is usually applied to any cat with stripes and bars. It has been claimed that if all the domestic cats in the world were to interbreed, eventually all cats would be tabbies. The 'M' on the forehead has been said to be the mark of Mohammed. The most common Tabby varieties are Brown, Red, Silver, Blue, Cameo and Cream. RIGHT: A Brown Tabby Short-hair.

Every country has tales of cats that take human form or vice versa. In Japan, cats with long tails were said to have this power – which may either account for or be accounted for by the fact that the native cats of Japan have very short tails. In Japan too, black cats were considered good luck as they were thought able to cure disease especially in children, but red or pink cats were thought to have super-natural powers and were avoided.

During the fourteenth century the black cat was well known as either a witch or a devil in disguise, and these poor creatures took the brunt of the feline persecutions during the Dark Ages.

Today, however, whether or not one avoids black cats depends on where one lives. In the United States and Ireland the old superstitions persist, and a black cat crossing one's path always means bad luck.

But in England and Scotland black cats bring good luck. English sailors purchased them for their wives, believing that as long as the cat was contented the weather would be fair, and in Scotland a black cat in the house ensured that the young ladies who lived there would have plenty of beaux.

Black cats are also considered good luck in the Orient. Chinese sailors carried them aboard ship to bring favorable winds.

A Cream Short-hair kitten. Cream Short-hairs are beautiful and much-admired cats, but are very difficult to breed to standard. The body conformation should be that of the Short-hair. Kittens are often born with barred markings which they may or may not lose as they mature. Bars, stripes, and especially ringed tails are the most common fault in adult animals.

*A Sable or Brown Burmese. Burmese cats
(called Zibelines in France) were developed in
the United States and can be traced back to a
single female that arrived in New Orleans in 1930
in the company of a sailor. Burmese are hardy,
sociable cats that make good companions and
tend to be 'possessive' about their families.
The Sable Burmese has a close-lying, satin-
textured coat of a deep, rich, warm sable
brown that gradually becomes slightly lighter on
the underparts. Otherwise the color is even.*

Cats in the Arts

Cats in Literature

Cats and writers seem to have an affinity for each other, and the list of famous writers who owned, were fond of, and in many cases, wrote about cats would be long indeed. From Lord Byron to Mark Twain, from Henry James to Ernest Hemingway, Dickens, Wordsworth, Baudelaire – the names span the history of poetry and prose on every continent.

During medieval times animal stories were very popular, as they had always been – and still are today. Many of these stories were collected into *Bestiaries*, collections of descriptions of the habits of various animals, each followed by a 'signification' that derived a Christian moral from the story. One of the few fragments remaining of the Anglo-Saxon *Physiologus* is the story of the Panther, and the more complete Middle English *Beastiary* contains 'The Lion.'

The first text devoted entirely to the domestic cat appeared during the latter half of the sixteenth century. Chaucer mused on the cat's preference for mice over milk in *The Manciple's Tale*.

Cats pop in and out of literature for the next three centuries, gradually becoming more likeable as time goes on. Cervantes has Don Quixote accuse a group of cats of witchcraft – a reference to the horrors of the Middle Ages, as is the witches' invocation of Graymalkin in *Macbeth*. In John Gay's fable 'The Rat-Catcher and Cats' the two factions eventually arrive at a working agreement. There are three rather important cats in Dicken's *Bleak House* (1852), belonging to Krook, Mr Jellyby and Mr Vohles. And who could forget Dinah in *Alice in Wonderland* or the Cheshire Cat in *Through the Looking Glass*?

Cats play starring roles in many more modern works by famous writers. Even the briefest list would have to include Kipling's *The Cat That Walked By Himself*; Poe's masterpiece of horror, *The Black Cat*; Hemingway's short story, *Cat in the Rain*; *The Cat* by Collette; and *The Malediction* by Tennessee Williams; not to mention *archy and mehitabel* by don marquis; and a number of excellent books by Paul Gallico.

Poets have been no less inspired by their pets: Thomas Gray wrote *Ode* in 1742; Horace Walpole's unfortunate cat Selima drowned in a tub of goldfish; Edward Lear immortalized the marriage of *The Owl and the Pussycat*. Wordsworth, Blake (The Tyger), Yeats, Swinburne, and Hardy are just a few of the many others whose cats moved them to poetry.

The poetry of T S Eliot is justly famous for its erudition and social consciousness, but not often for its humor. In *Old Possum's Book of Practical Cats*, however, he reveals an entirely new side of his character in a witty, but always thoroughly sympathetic and knowledgable series of poems about cats.

OPPOSITE: A Lynx Point (also known as Silver Point Siamese, Shadow Point, and Tabby Colorpoint Short-hair). Lynx Points tend to have gentle natures. BELOW: The Oriental Lavendar, sometimes called the Foreign Lilac.

The poems address two very important topics, *The Naming of Cats* ('. . . a difficult matter, (that) isn't just one of your holiday games') and *The Ad-dressing of Cats*.

We are then introduced to a number of cats, all of whom are immediately recognizable. There is the Gumbie Cat, the tabby 'on whom well-ordered households depend . . .' and the Rum Tum Tugger, a perverse animal who '. . . will do as he do do and there's no doing anything about it!' The rather small, black and white Jellicle Cats rest up all day so that they can dance all night; the Great Rumpus Cat single-handedly routs a whole army of Pekes and Pollicles; Mr Mistoffelees, the original Conjuring Cat, not only spirits away various household items, but magically produces seven kittens. Maccivity, the 'Napoleon of Crime' baffles Scotland Yard while Gus the theater cat reminisces about his past triumphs on the boards. Bustopher Jones saunters toward one or another of his clubs in St James's and Skimbleshanks rides the Midnight Mail. And last, but never least, is Growltiger, a bargee known as 'The Terror of the Thames' who is finally forced to walk the plank by a gang of dastardly Siamese.

Furthermore, one of the best examples of indirectly using cat images to establish a mood is a stanza in T S Eliot's *The Love Song of J Alfred Prufrock*.

The study of cat literature *per se* can be a time-consuming but rewarding occupation. Anyone seriously interested in pursuing the topic would be well advised to consult Claire Necker's *Four Centuries of Cat Books, 1570–1970*, published by Scarecrow Press in 1972 – an annotated bibliography of cat books published in English.

The range in cat literature is enormous. There are adventurous cats like Dick Whittington's friend or Puss in Boots, and there are long-suffering cats as in Susannah Patteson's *Pussy Meow*. There are musical cats (*The King of Cats* by Stephen Vincent Benet), talking cats (*Tobermory* by Saki) and even cats who are FBI agents (*Undercover Cat* by The Gordons).

The Cornish Si-Rex is the result of the mating of a Cornish Rex cat and a Siamese cat.

The largest number of cat books are written for children; the next largest subdivision covers cat care. There are also many general cat books (of which Agnes Repplier's *The Fireside Sphynx*, first published in 1901, is an excellent example), fiction, anthologies, picture books, cartoon books, and scientific books – anything in short, that strikes a reader's fancy.

Cats in Art

People have been drawing, painting, and sculpturing cats since the time of the ancient Egyptians. Often they were symbols of freedom and independence; cats appeared on the shields of Roman soldiers, on the coat of arms of the Dukes of Burgundy, and as symbols of freedom both in Holland during the Dutch struggle for

independence in the sixteenth century, and again during the French Revolution.

During the thirteenth century the example of St Francis of Assisi led to many sympathetic portrayals of cats especially by Italian painters. Around 1450, the philosopher St Jerome was depicted with a feline companion by Antonello da Messino. But just as often cats represented evil. Ghirlandaio, Luini, and Cellini all painted Judas accompanied by a cat; St Ives, the patron saint of lawyers, was often shown with a cat said to represent all the

OPPOSITE: *The Oriental or Foreign Short-hair is similar in conformation to the Siamese cat, but has the colorpoints eliminated. The cat here is an Oriental or Foreign Smoke.* ABOVE: *An Oriental Lavendar Queen and her kittens.*

The two most popular types of Burmese cats. On the left is a Sable or Brown Burmese and on the right is a Blue Burmese. Depending on the geneology of the cats involved, both colors can occur in the same litter as can any of the other varieties of Burmese cats.

evil qualities associated with that profession. In Dürer's engraving *Adam and Eve* (1504) the cat is a cruel symbol. Da Vinci's study of the cat however, reveals a scientific exploration of the cat's form.

In 1523 Guilio Romano would paint a threatening evil cat in *Madonna della Gatta*, but by the end of the century Federico Barocci was showing cats in a much more naturalistic manner – in, for example, *Holy Cat With Family* (1574) and *Annunciation* (1584). Cats were residents of the Garden of Eden in Breughel the Elder's *Paradise* in the early 1600s.

From that point on, the treatment of cats in western painting became increasingly sympathetic and naturalistic. Some of the most charming portrayals of cats include Jan Steen's *The Cat's Reading Lesson* (1650), Jean Baptiste Greuze's *The Wool Winder* (1759), Renoir's *Woman With A Cat* (1880) and Mary Cassatt's *Children Playing With a Cat* (1908).

Several artists in both east and west have achieved a certain measure of popularity by drawing or painting cats.

Gottfried Mind, a Swiss artist, became known as the 'Cat Raphael' in Europe at the beginning of the nineteenth century for his drawings and water colors that are almost photographic reproductions of the animals he loved.

During the mid-1800s, a Japanese artist named Kuniyoshi produced many portraits of cats that show both understanding and humor. His cats range from anthropomorphic representations (*The Cat Family at Home*, c.1840) to demons (*The Cat Witch of Okabe*), to realistic studies (*Cats for the Fifty-Three Stations of Tokaido Road*, 1848).

RIGHT: *The ever-popular Blue Burmese cat.*
BELOW: *This Siamese kitten is similar in type to the Burmese cat, but with a less solid body and more pointed face.*

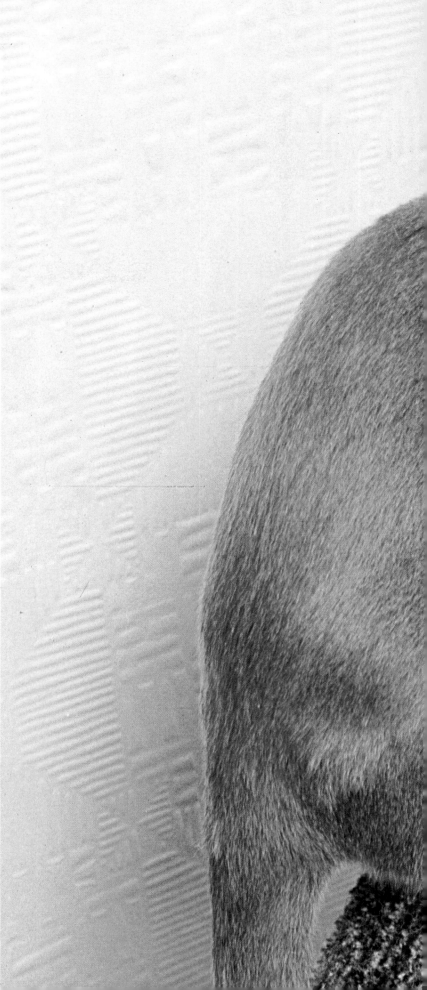

In England at the end of the century Louis Wain was an enormously popular illustrator whose drawings of cats appeared in countless children's books, magazines, and newspapers on both sides of the Atlantic. Unfortunately he went mad and was committed to an asylum in 1924. His popularity continued, but gradually his style changed until his drawings became more concerned with patterns than with accurate representations of cats. Today he is remembered by many for the way in which he helped popularize cats, and is also famous in psychiatry for the manner in which his growing schizophrenia expressed itself in his art.

Cats in Music

Cats have appeared in western music for many centuries. Songs about cats abound – children's songs, famous cat poems that have been set to music, and others like that most popular cat song of all, 'The Cat Came Back.'

Many instrumental pieces have been inspired by cats. Scarlatti and Liszt both composed pieces titled *The Cat's Fugue*, while Chopin produced the *Cat Valse*. Stravinsky wrote *Lullabies for the Cat*. Prokofiev used sensuous woodwinds to denote the cat in *Peter and the Wolf*, while Zey Confrey imitated a cat running over

OPPOSITE: *A Blue Burmese. This color was achieved by mating the lighter-colored kittens from a Sable Burmese litter and the required conformation is the same as for the Sable Burmese.*

ABOVE: *A Rex kitten. It has a curly coat.*

the piano in his jazz classic, *Kitten on the Keys*.

Tschaikovsky's famous ballet *The Sleeping Beauty* contains a famous scene in which two dancers, Puss in Boots and White Cat, imitate feline movements; there are many other dances inspired by cats, and ballet has even named one of its most difficult steps – the *pas de chat* – after them.

No one knows how much cats like human music, but some have certainly been active in the music world. Jenny Lind, for example, used to sing to her pet cat. Saint Saens was a noted cat lover, and Albert Schweitzer was seldom seen without a feline companion.

Havana Brown kittens enjoying their meal. These affectionate, soft-voiced cats make admirable pets. They often have the unusual habit of using their paws to investigate strange objects by touch, rather than relying on their sense of smell as do most other breeds. Havanas are generally healthy animals, but suffer in the cold.

Cats Today

In many ways many cats lead better lives today than ever before. As the human standard of living rises, so does that of those pets lucky enough to have secured a seat on the gravy train. In America or Europe today, a domestic cat who has a home is likely to have a very comfortable one. The usefulness of cats in advertising and the enormous number of books about them published each year mirror the important place they hold in society's affections. The ever-increasing number of pet boutiques, specialist shops and cemeteries, also indicates their growing status in the eyes of their owners.

Unfortunately this happy picture only applies to a very few of the world's cats. In America alone more than 50 million kittens are born each year – but only a very small number live more than a few months. Millions die of cold, hunger, disease, or injuries. Millions more are put down in one of the nation's 2000 public shelters or pounds, simply because there are no facilities to keep them for more than 48 or 72 hours. Some will even be sold to laboratories in a desperate attempt to raise money to provide shelter to others. The fate of the kittens who are born strays is hard enough to contemplate. The thought of those callously abandoned in rubbish cans or on the roadside by their owners – who thought it cruel or found it inconvenient to have their pets neutered – is horrible.

Wild cats find themselves in an equally unhappy though opposite situation. There is scarcely an entry for a wild cat in Section 3 (the Catalog Section) of this book that does not note that the species is in grave danger of extinction – either from intensive hunting, or from more impersonal threats such as the destruction of the animals' habitat through war or the encroachment of civilization. Zoos labor manfully to prevent the total extinction of many rare breeds, but all too often the end result is that the number of animals of a given species becomes restricted to but a few kept in captivity.

Cat lovers, then, have two battles to fight: overpopulation on the domestic front and declining population in the wild. Neither will be won easily, or quickly, or cheaply.

OPPOSITE: A Blue Persian, or Blue Long-hair. ABOVE: A Long-hair Colorpoint, or Himalayan. BELOW: This Blue Colorpoint kitten is often called a Blue Point Himalayan. Both names are acceptable. OVERLEAF: A Chinchilla, sometimes called a Silver Persian.

Cat Care

Choosing Your Cat

There are as many reasons for getting a cat as there are people. Some want a companion, others a mouser. Some are concerned with teaching their children about the facts of life and giving them responsibility. For others, cats are a fascinating (and sometimes expensive) hobby.

One of the first decisions that must be made after you have decided to acquire a cat is whether you want a pedigree animal or an ordinary one (if there is any such thing as an 'ordinary' cat!).

OPPOSITE AND BELOW: Chinchilla (Silver Persian) kittens. OVERLEAF: Blue Cream Persian.

If you are shopping for a pedigree cat, you can obtain lists of breeders by contacting your local cat club, checking various cat magazines, or by attending a cat show. Do not be afraid to shop around; prices of both purebred pets and show animals vary widely. If you are not familiar with a breed it is a good idea to go to several shows and/or get expert advice before committing yourself to a large expenditure.

If you are not concerned about your cat's family tree, the list of sources is almost inexhaustible. Friends, the newspapers, open-air markets, and even the street itself are all places to find free cats. Humane societies have more cats than they can handle, and you can adopt one for a minimum fee that covers vaccinations, etc. Pet stores often have kittens for sale.

Check your potential pet carefully. The cat's eyes should be clear and no white should show at the corners. The nostrils should be clear too – mucus is a sure sign of health problems. Ears should be clean, the fur should contain no fleas or flea eggs, and the skin should be free of sores and scabs.

Pet stores and breeders should provide a written list of any shots that have already been given, and most reputable establishments will also give you a health guarantee.

No matter how you obtain your cat, it should be taken to a veterinarian within the first two or three days so that any

problems it may have can be spotted early, and it can receive any necessary vaccinations and inoculations.

The sex of the new pet is also worth thinking about ahead of time, even if you have no strong prejudices one way or the other.

Unaltered male cats have an uncontrollable urge to roam in search of females, to fight for them if they find them, and to spray the house if they do not. Your knowledge of first aid will be severely tested if you have an unaltered male, and the smell of his urine, attractive though it might be to his lady friends, will certainly be repellant to you. Castrating or neutering your tom will remove his wanderlust and stop the spraying, but will probably not keep him from fighting.

In addition to the problem of disposing of unwanted litters, unspayed females can be a nuisance when they are in heat, as can their beaux.

It is difficult to put the case in favor of spaying or neutering too strongly. Hundreds of thousands of unwanted kittens are born each year, and to add to their number is simply madness.

Spaying should be done at as early an age as possible, preferably before the cat first comes into heat. Toms are usually neutered between the ages of six and eight months.

RIGHT AND BELOW: Chinchillas. Many people consider Chinchillas to be the most beautiful long-haired cat.

Daily Care of the Healthy Cat

Grooming

Although cats keep themselves reasonably clean, they sometimes need help – especially long-haired cats.

Bathing

There are times when cats get so dirty that a bath is the only solution. Whether it turns out to be a relatively painless experience for everyone or a battle royal depends on how well things are organized in advance.

The best place to bathe a cat is in a laundry tub or in the kitchen or bathroom sink. The bathtub is too low and too large to be convenient for you or comfortable for the cat. Place a rough towel or a rubber mat on the bottom of the sink to give the cat a foothold. Also needed are a large towel for drying the cat, shampoo (human baby shampoo is as good as the special cat shampoos), and vaseline.

Next, banish the children. Bathing is an unpleasant experience for the average cat under the best of circumstances, and a large noisy audience will not improve matters.

Fill the sink with warm water (80–90°F) to a depth of three to four inches. Smear vaseline around the cat's eyes for protection and stand it in the sink, holding it by the back of the neck. Hold it there for a few minutes, talking reassuringly. Then, working slowly and gently, pour water over it, followed by the shampoo. After a few minutes to allow the shampoo to loosen the dirt and grease, rinse the cat thoroughly. One soaping and rinsing is usually sufficient.

It is important to dry the cat well; use a rough towel vigorously and make sure the hair next to the skin is dry. Wipe the vaseline from the eyes and brush and comb out any loose hair. The cat should be kept indoors for five to six hours after a bath. For this reason it is probably best to bathe it at night and keep it indoors till morning. Kittens should only be bathed when absolutely necessary.

Brushing and Combing

Regular brushing and combing, on the order of two or three times a week, will vastly improve a cat's appearance and make it feel better as well.

A cat will enjoy the brushing session if it has grown accustomed to them as a kitten. Older cats may put up a struggle.

It is not necessary to spend a lot of money on grooming equipment for most cats; small combs and stiff brushes or grooming mits are available at pet stores at reasonable prices. Tweezers and blunt-edged scissors are also useful for dealing with mats and snarls.

Starting at the head, brush in one direction. Work quietly and gently, remembering that too heavy a hand will only irritate the cat and make it less willing to be brushed next time.

Claws

Provided that a cat receives the proper amount of exercise and is provided with a scratching post, its nails should not require trimming whether the cat is an outdoor cat or an indoor cat.

Should a cat's nails become too long for some reason, it is advisable to take it to a veterinarian to have its claws clipped. However, if this is impractical then special clippers are available from pet stores – scissors should be avoided except in an emergency.

To clip a cat's claws place your thumb just above the cat's toe and your index finger on the pad beneath. When finger and thumb are pressed together the claw will extend; clip it just where it begins to curve. *Never* clip the pink area of the claw; it is better to clip too little than too much. If you do happen to clip into the quick and the claw starts to bleed, use an antiseptic powder or spray, apply a compress or clean handkerchief, and hold the paw up for a few minutes until the bleeding stops.

A scratching post is a must, and it is probably better to try a homemade one first. A four-foot post with rough bark (or covered with carpet) on a heavy wooden base will do. It should be placed in a corner where the cat can get at it easily. A

OPPOSITE: A Tortoiseshell Persian (or Long-hair). The coat of this striking cat is long and patterned with distinct patches of deep, rich black, red, and cream. Black is not predominant. It is virtually an all-female breed. The few males born are sterile.

50

toy mouse on a spring attached to the top will give the cat more exercise.

Declawing is the subject of a major controversy; veterinarians and cat owners alike disagree about the relative advantages and disadvantages of the procedure. It is not our intention here to make a stand one way or the other. Plenty of literature is available in cat magazines and from veterinarians, and each cat owner must make the ultimate decision about what is best for his or her pet.

Eyes
Cats' eyes usually do not require much care beyond an occasional trim if the hair around the eyes is getting into them. This should be done very carefully if not by a veterinarian.

Ears
Cats' ears should be examined regularly. Wax can accumulate in the ears but it is fairly easy to remove with a cotton swab after softening with warm mineral oil. Go gently and carefully, since a cat's ears are very sensitive. Ear mites and other ear ailments should be referred to a veterinarian.

Teeth and Gums
While it is not necessary to brush a cat's teeth regularly, brushing does help reduce the build-up of tartar. Massaging the gums with salt water will slow down the growth of bacteria and also help stop bad breath. If a lot of tartar has built up, it is best to let a veterinarian remove it.

Hazards

There is a certain amount of danger associated with the very act of living and functioning in the outside world. For cats, as for small children, however, many potential hazards can be eliminated or their likelihood decreased by simply giving some thought in advance to their environment.

Heights
Cats can, and often do, fall from high places – and their famed ability to land on their feet cannot always save them from serious injury. It should be a standard household rule not to play with the cat near an unprotected window or on roofs, fire escapes, or balconies. Screens on all windows are a good idea; they are good safety devices for children and everyone else in the family, as well as making the windowsill a safe place from which the cat can watch the world go by.

Cats 'stuck' in trees generally manage to get down by themselves sooner or later – sooner if they are left alone to figure out how to do it themselves. People making a scene under the tree usually only convince the cat that it is better off staying put. On those rare occasions when the cat really needs help, the fire department or humane society is probably better qualified to give it than you are.

Electricity
Electrical wires and telephone cords can be irresistible – and very dangerous – playthings. Lamp cords should be run along the walls or under rugs whenever possible. Powdered alum or bitter aloes can be used to coat electrical cords if a cat persists in chewing on them.

Collars
It is possible to find a safe collar, but it sometimes takes some looking. Fit is all-important: if the collar is too loose it can catch on bushes or fences; if too tight it can choke the cat. Flea collars are sometimes useful.

Enclosed Places
The list of places that cats can be shut into when one is not paying attention is virtually endless – drawers, cupboards, closets, refrigerators, trunks, and boxes are only a few. If your cat is missing, start by checking the refrigerator (as the most dangerous spot), and continue around the house from there.

Poisons
All household cleaning agents, paints, insecticides, and of course all drugs and medicines should be kept up high behind closed doors for the safety of both cats and children.

People
Cats who are allowed outdoors always run some risk of meeting one of those unfortunate people who enjoy hurting small

A White Persian (or White Long-hair). The Persian is the aristocrat of domestic cats. Many experts believe that it first appeared in Persia and Turkey, and is the descendant of some type of Asian wild cat.

animals and there is nothing much anyone can do to prevent it. But cats also run some risk from people in their own home – usually when their owner is carrying something large and heavy and inadvertently trips over them. The best way to avoid this is to make sure the animal is in another part of the house, or outside, when there is carrying to be done – and to feed it first, since hungry cats are much more likely to be under foot.

Children can often be hazards – usually through ignorance, but occasionally when they vent aggressions on the family pet that they cannot safely take out on their parents or siblings. Children should be taught respect for animals firmly and at an early age – for their own sake as well as for the animal's.

Feeding
See also Nutrition.

Most adult domestic cats prefer to eat once or twice a day, like their larger cousins. But unlike wild cats who must take their meals as they find them house pets soon become creatures of habit and prefer to be fed at the same time in the same place.

The cat's food dish should be placed somewhere out of the way, where the animal can eat in peace without being tripped over or harassed by small children. Cats like to drag their food out of the bowl, so put newspaper or a rubber mat under the feeding dish if you care about your floors.

Cool, clean water should be available at all times.

Food should be served at room temperature. Cats like to take their time over their meal; leave the food for about an hour, then remove whatever has not been eaten.

If a cat misses more than two or three meals in a row it is either (1) being fed

somewhere else; (2) hunting; or (3) sick. If you can eliminate (1) and (2) as possibilities, take the cat to a veterinarian.

Here is a sample test for obesity: you should be able to feel your cat's ribs, but not see them. If you can see the ribs, the animal is too thin; if you cannot even feel them, it is too fat.

Nutrition
See also Feeding.
Although not much is known about the cat's exact nutritional requirements, it is obvious that a well-balanced diet is essential to its health. This is especially important for the house cat, who is completely dependent on its owner for food.

Cats are complete carnivores; as such they need large quantities of fat and protein (much more, proportionally, than dogs) and few carbohydrates.

Commercial Pet Food
Pet owners have raised healthy cats without prepared food for thousands of years, but it cannot be denied that commercial pet foods make the average cat-owner's life much easier. They are also safer than hunting, since mice and other prey could contain tapeworm or other parasites.

It is well worth paying a few extra pennies for good-quality cat food, if only to ensure that your pet is not eating a mixture that is mostly cereal (or in some cases, sawdust). Most countries require that cat foods labeled 'complete' or 'balanced' be able to support a normal adult animal as its sole source of nourishment.

A Balinese cat and her kitten. The Balinese is basically a long-haired Siamese. Like the Siamese, they are highly intelligent and affectionate cats.

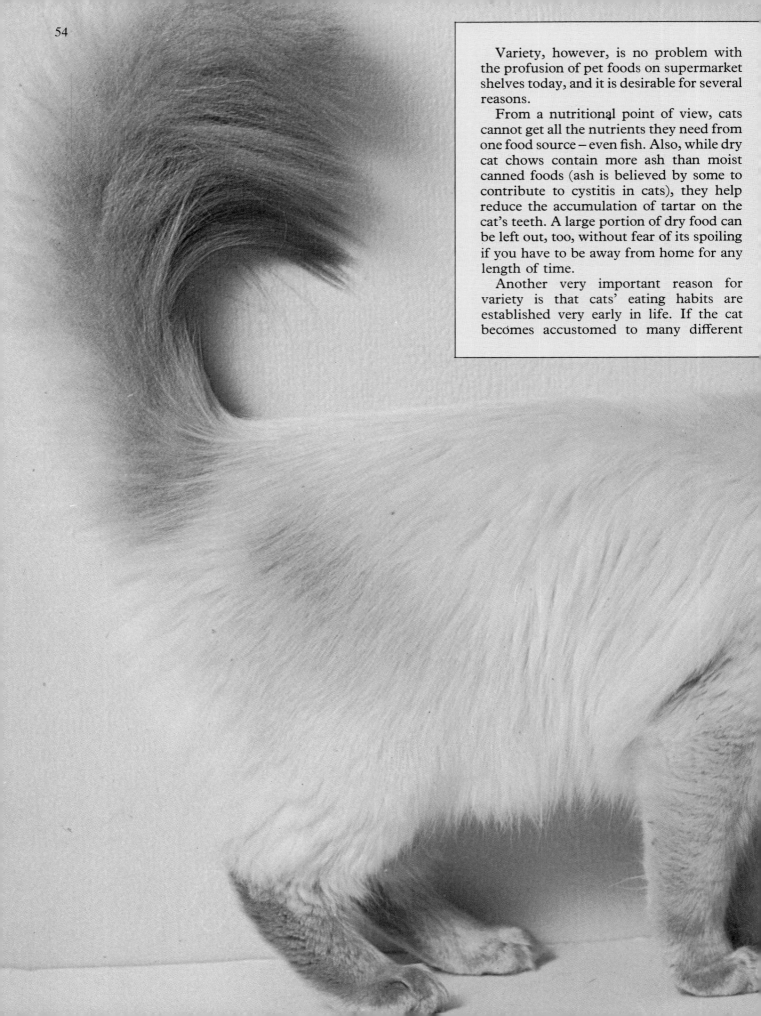

Variety, however, is no problem with the profusion of pet foods on supermarket shelves today, and it is desirable for several reasons.

From a nutritional point of view, cats cannot get all the nutrients they need from one food source – even fish. Also, while dry cat chows contain more ash than moist canned foods (ash is believed by some to contribute to cystitis in cats), they help reduce the accumulation of tartar on the cat's teeth. A large portion of dry food can be left out, too, without fear of its spoiling if you have to be away from home for any length of time.

Another very important reason for variety is that cats' eating habits are established very early in life. If the cat becomes accustomed to many different types and textures in its food it will be much easier for it to accept special diets which may become necessary when the animal is older or ill.

A normally active adult cat should thrive on one-half to one can of moist food a day, chow (and water) to snack on, table scraps, grass, and whatever else can be found during a day of wandering.

Fresh Food

If you prefer to prepare your cat's food yourself, a few logical rules should suffice.

Meat can be eaten raw (except pork); avoid spicy or cured meats like ham and salami, and be sure to provide a good balance between beef, lamb, horse, and chicken. Fish should be cooked and the bones ground if possible. Vegetables should always be cooked as well. Many cats cannot digest egg whites easily, but hardboiled egg yolks are good occasional diet supplements. Skim milk is better for cats than whole.

Other Pets

There are so many stories of devoted friendships between dogs and cats that it hardly needs saying: there is no reason why the two species cannot live together in near-perfect harmony.

This is especially true if the animals have been brought up together from childhood. Introducing a cat (especially a

A Blue Point Balinese cat. Balinese cats should not be confused with Persian cats or Himalayan cats, which have much longer coats.

mature one) into a home where there is already an adult dog (or vice versa) requires more tact and patience, as the two work out territorial disputes, jealousy, competition for food, and so on. Your own reading of your dog's character and temperament will have to tell you whether you can acquire a cat at all or if it should be a kitten or an adult. In any case, as with children, you will have to keep a sharp eye out until the two have come to some sort of truce based on mutual respect. Go as slowly as necessary; trying to force the friendship never works. You may even have to keep the two in separate rooms for awhile until they get used to the idea of another animal in the house.

Birds are a different story. About the best you can do is keep the cage out of reach and away from launching pads as much as possible, install a cat-proof latch (if any have been invented yet), and allow the bird out only when you are certain that the cat is outdoors. Some cats become accustomed to pet birds and virtually ignore them; others never give up the hunt.

Pet mammals (hamsters, gerbils, mice, etc), fish, and small reptiles will probably be irresistible. Again, cages should have strong locks; aquariums should be covered with heavy glass, and terrariums with heavy wire mesh.

Sanitation

Litter boxes are absolutely necessary for house-bound cats, and it is a good idea to keep one handy for outdoor cats as well.

Aluminum or stainless steel litter trays are more expensive than plastic, but they are more durable, are easier to keep clean, and do not absorb odors. The box should be large enough for the cat to turn around in, and should be at least two inches deep.

The pan should be placed somewhere that is accessible but private, and out of the way of household traffic and children.

A commercial litter, sand, or gravel is the best for the sanitary pan. Sawdust, peat moss, peanut shells, or shredded newspaper can also be used. Litter should be about two inches deep.

A dirty litter pan will begin to annoy your cat long before it annoys you. Litter (or at least the soiled litter) should be

OPPOSITE: A Cream Persian or Long-hair. This popular variety originated from crossing Blues and Reds.

removed and replaced every day. The pan should be washed once a week with hot water and detergent. Perfumed detergents and disinfectant sprays will probably annoy the cat and can make it stop using the pan altogether. Read the labels on disinfectants carefully to make sure they are safe.

Training

Many people believe that cats cannot be trained at all. In a sense this is true. Cats are certainly as intelligent as most other animals, but they are not about to be coaxed, teased, or especially threatened into doing what you want them to do. Nor will they go out of their way to behave in a certain way just to please you.

Dr Benjamin Hart notes that cats are the only animals except for primates who learn by observation. Cats who have had many opportunities to watch others open a latched door, for example, often figure out how to do it themselves.

Cats can, however, be manipulated into the sort of behavior you desire if they believe it is in their own best interests. The quality required to implement this manipulation is confidence. And remember that there is no such thing as 'uncatlike behavior' – if you do not train your cat it will certainly train you.

Especially in the beginning, use a high-pitched voice to get the cat's attention Physical maltreatment should be avoided. Often effective with other pets, it usually only makes a cat want to fight back or escape.

Collars and Other Accessories

Cats will tolerate collars, leashes, and harnesses only if these were introduced when they were kittens. Sometimes, however, they are a necessity – for example, if you live in a community that requires cats to wear identification.

Collars can be very dangerous (Hazards, page 50). The best kind to buy is an all-elastic safety collar that is not tight enough to choke the animal and not so loose that it falls off or catches on protruding objects.

If you want to use a leash, buy one of leather, with a swivel hook, and let the cat smell it and play with it a bit before attaching it to the collar. With patience, and the knowledge that the cat will probably never walk sedately at your side for more than a few steps, you and your pet will eventually

come to a compromise where you allow it the freedom to wander back and forth while it walks when you want to walk instead of balking.

Harnesses are usually used for walking larger cats such as ocelots. They should be snug but not tight. If necessary, pad the straps that go across the chest.

Coming When Called

Teaching your cat to come when you call will save you an incalculable amount of aggravation when it is time for feeding, grooming, or locking up for the night.

The procedure is a simple one. Get the cat's attention by calling its name (a falsetto voice will probably work best). Then offer it an irresistible treat – a sardine, brewer's yeast tablet, bowl of chocolate ice cream, or whatever. When it comes over to you, give it the treat and a lot of praise.

After many iterations you will have established a Pavlovian reaction and the cat will come running whenever it hears its name. It is not a good idea to tap the bowl on the floor as you call; you will never be sure which of the sounds the cat associates with the food – and it is uncomfortable standing outside at midnight, in the dead of winter, desperately tapping on a little plastic bowl.

While this technique works with many cats, many others will refuse to be manipulated. Even the experts fail sometimes. Confidence and persistence still give you a pretty good chance of success.

Obeying the House Rules

Whenever you acquire a new cat it will have to learn the 'house rules' – that some chairs or sofas are off limits, that the dining room table and kitchen counter are for-

A Birman adult and a kitten. Legend says that the Birman (also called the Sacred Cat of Burma) guarded temples in ancient times in Burma.

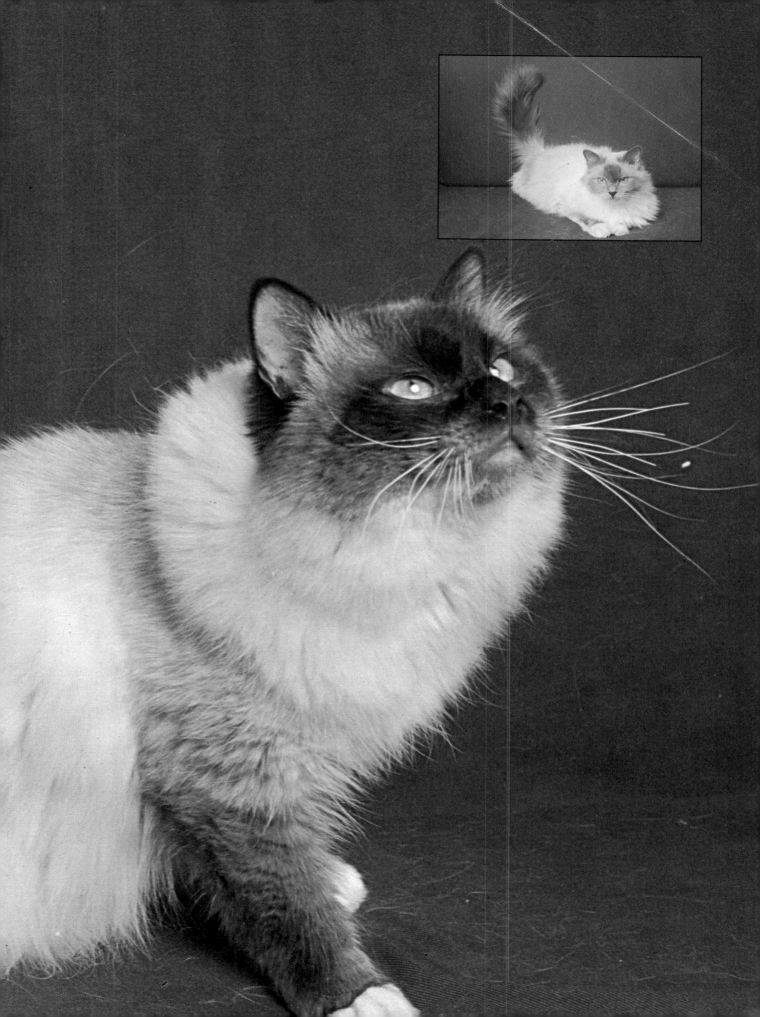

bidden territory, that furniture is not for scratching nor drapes for climbing nor plants for eating, and so on.

Scolding is often enough to let a kitten know that it has misbehaved. If that does not work, a sudden loud noise is often effective – hand clapping or smacking a table with a rolled-up newspaper. The next stage might well be a toy squirt gun or spray water bottle. If a cat persists in clawing carpets or drapes, it may be necessary to trim its front claws.

Some misbehavior stems from *your* failure to provide acceptable alternatives. For example, a cat needs to sharpen its claws, and in the absence of a scratching post will generally use the nearest chair or carpet. Kittens are easily trained to use a post; with older cats a little catnip on or around it will help attract the animal.

Boredom is another reason for misbehavior. Be sure that the cat has some things around that can provide permissible diversions. Paper bags, empty thread spools, and stuffed socks are good, safe, inexpensive playthings.

Some cats misbehave to punish their owners – usually in a way nicely calculated to infuriate them. (I once had a cat who would mess in the middle of the bath mat whenever she felt she had been unfairly scolded or had not been given enough attention.)

Again, confidence and persistence must be your watchwords coupled with vigilance and *consistency*. You cannot expect a cat to be anything but confused if you allow it to sleep in a certain chair one day and reprimand it for doing so the next.

Litter Box
It is very easy to teach a cat to use a litter tray. Since cats instinctively prefer to urinate and defecate in a sandy place where they can cover up their excreta, they will usually take to the litter pan almost immediately.

Mother cats usually teach their kittens to use a litter tray, but sometimes a kitten will get confused, or find what it thinks is a better spot – a large potted plant, for instance. A few days spent keeping a close eye on the kitten, picking it up and placing it in the sanitary pan at the first hint of trouble, should solve the problem.

If an older cat starts refusing to use the pan, make sure the litter is clean and that the pan is placed somewhere accessible, yet private. Male cats sometimes refuse the tray when they are sexually aroused, and some sick cats cannot use it. In these cases, keep the cat in one room with newspapers on the floor.

Cats have been taught to use the toilet successfully. One procedure, described by Benjamin L Hart in an article for *Feline Practice* (and reprinted in *Cat Catalog*) is as follows.

1 Keep the regular litter tray in the bathroom until the cat is used to the location.

2 Remove the regular tray and make a new one. Cut a cardboard rim the size of the toilet seat, cover it with clear plastic material, and attach it by wires to the underside of the seat. When filled with litter, the toilet seat is the edge of the 'litter box' and the plastic is the bottom. Of course, this means that the humans in the house must use another toilet for awhile.

3 The cat should be used to its new litter box in a few days, and will probably already be balancing itself on the toilet seat (since the plastic bottom feels very insecure). At this point, reduce the amount of litter by about half.

4 Over the next few days, continue to reduce the amount of litter, making holes in the plastic for urine to drip through, until finally you remove all the litter and the plastic. If you remove the litter too quickly and the cat stops using the toilet seat, go back to an earlier stage and go through the removal process again.

5 Expect the cat to fall in at least once. This may then mean that you have to go back to litter-and-plastic and go through the training process all over.

6 Some cats try to switch to the bathtub. Keeping an inch or two of water in the tub for a few days is an easy way to discourage this practice.

Cats and House Plants
Keeping both house cats and house plants at the same time can be a problem – as anyone who has come home from work to find their favorite *Coleus* chewed to a frazzle knows only too well.

No one is quite sure why cats eat plants. Boredom, say some. As roughage, or as an enemic, say others. Whatever the reason, it is something that is best stopped, not only to spare the feelings of the harassed

A Shaded Silver Persian. This type of cat is hard to differentiate from darker-than-average Chinchillas and lighter-than-average Shaded Silver Long-hairs.

cat/plant lover, but because many popular house plants are very poisonous to cats. Plants to watch out for include ivy, philodendron, daffodil and hyacinth foliage, Christmas cherry, and mistletoe.

No determined cat worth its salt will be foiled by elementary tricks like arranging plants close together (just knock a few pots off to make room on the shelf) or hanging them from the ceiling (great practice for the running high jump!) But spray repellants from pet stores will deter most cats.

Another solution, that does not deprive the cat of its late afternoon snack, might be to give it its own plants to munch. Grass seed is readily available and easy to grow, but many cats prefer meatier plants like wheat or oats. Have two or three pots growing in rotation so that a supply is always available.

For cats (especially kittens) who prefer your large plant tubs to their litter tray, try a repellant, or perhaps a layer of heavy pebbles with a dash of cayenne pepper.

Tricks

Cats *can* be taught to do tricks – if they feel like it and decide that there is something in it for them. The best technique to use is called 'shaping' – which simply means reinforcing the behavior you want.

For example, suppose you want to teach your cat to sit up. Wait until it comes up one day and puts its paws on your lap. Say 'sit up' in a pleased tone, perhaps moving your knees away and letting it balance with its front paws on your palms. Then reward it immediately. Continue this repetition of command and reward for closer and closer approximations to sitting up unassisted. After the cat has the idea, do *not* reward it for sitting up without the command.

When the trick has been well learned, you can begin rewarding the animal every other time it performs, then every third, every fourth, and so on, until you are rewarding on a random basis about every ten times. This will actually make the reinforcement stronger.

This same technique can be used to teach your cat to shake hands, fetch, or perform any other trick (that is not too undignified).

A Smoke Cameo. Cameos are attractive long-haired cats that were developed in America in the 1950s.

INDEX

ACKNOWLEDGMENTS

The author and publisher would like to thank the following
people who have helped in the preparation of this book:
Anistatia Vassilopoulos, who designed it; Thomas G
Aylesworth, who edited it; Karin Knight, who prepared the
index.

PICTURE CREDITS

Anne Cumbers: 8–9, 15 (inset), 24, 28, 29, 35 (inset), 38,
    45, 46, 47, 52–53, 54–55, 60.
Geoffrey Kinns: 6.
Orbis: 1, 4–5, 11, 25, 26–27, 30, 31, 32, 33, 36–37, 39,
    40–41, 42, 43, 48, 57, 58–59.
Sally Anne Thompson: 2, 7, 10, 12–13, 14–15, 16–17, 18,
    19, 20–21, 22–23, 34–35, 51, 62–63.